BUCKINGHAMSHIRE

A portrait in colour

———

ANDY WILLIAMS & JEAN ARCHER

COUNTRYSIDE BOOKS

First Published 1994
© Andy Williams 1994

COUNTRYSIDE BOOKS
3 CATHERINE ROAD
NEWBURY, BERKSHIRE

ISBN 1 85306 278 2

Cover design by Mon Mohan
Produced through MRM Associates Ltd., Reading
Typset by Paragon Typesetters, Queensferry
Printed by Ian Allan Printing Ltd., Addlestone

Contents

INTRODUCTION

A colour photographer of calibre such as Andy Williams must surely find a wealth of material in the County of Buckingham with its diversity of scenery which divides naturally into four areas. There are the languid slopes of the Thames Valley, the robust Chilterns, the Aylesbury Vale or Plain, and the vast expanse of North Bucks.

The rolling beech woods of the Chilterns in spring offer delicate shades of lush green, a floor of bluebells dotted with rays of sunlight, and wild cherry billowing here and there. In the autumn, Buckinghamshire woodlands blaze with yellows, gold and copper red. There is colour in the hedgerows of the lanes, and red brick cottages (white walled or ochre coloured wychert in mid-Bucks), have gardens bursting with flowers. Towns and villages all play their part for the photographer, offering atmosphere and contrast as well as colour.

In the summertime, there is also a deep beauty in the shade of streets and alleyways of towns, regal administration buildings and Market Halls. There are glorious mellow hues to ancient manor houses such as Chenies, Shardeloes and Marsh Gibbon, as well as stately homes at Waddesdon, Claydon, Cliveden and the magnificent ornamental grounds of Stowe.

Cattle stand knee deep in wild flowers in the water meadows of the River Thame, and birds 'rule the roost'. Other rivers and streams – the Ouse at Olney and its offshoot the Ousel, the Wye, the Hamble, the Misbourne and the Chess idle their way through heavenly valleys.

The long panoramic views from Ivinghoe Beacon and Coombe Hill give wide ranges of colour receding into the blue distance. Walking is always a joy, whether it is along the Icknield Way and the Ridgeway, or past windmills, over bridges, and even beside ponds.

For some centuries Buckinghamshire maintained a low population until the coming of the Metropolitan Railway towards the end of the last century. Then, some towns such as Amersham and Beaconsfield evaded the expansion and growth that came with it by establishing new centres around the railway station. During the first half of this century, Metroland spread out alongside the track, affecting places like Little Chalfont, and Chesham Bois. Neat suburban settings replaced fields, along the line up to Aylesbury and beyond.

This influx increased during and since the last war, and has led in part to the loss of the Buckinghamshire dialect, especially in the south of the county where, being close to a widening London, it has been blended and diluted with the language of the newcomers. Yet it can still be discerned in the vowels of a native, and the odd word emerges that is peculiar only to Bucks.

The county has inspired artists and writers in colourful array – Shelley and Peacock at Marlow, Gray at Stoke Poges, Milton at Chalfont St Giles, Waller at Coleshill, Cowper at Olney, Rupert Brook, Robert Louis Stevenson, John Masefield, G K Chesterton, and Alison Uttley who wrote her own superb book on Buckinghamshire.

The people have a proud record of giving support to the rebel and the underdog. John Wycliffe and his Lollard followers found not only support here, but also a fervent adherence to their cause by people who were willing to be burned at the stake for ideas of religious freedom. Thomas Harding at Chesham was one and there were William Tylesworth and others at Amersham.

The Quakers Isaac Pennington, Thomas Ellwood and friends found and loved this area. Their oldest Meeting Houses were built in Bucks, such as Jordans, where the great William Penn, founder of Pennsylvania is buried.

Neither has the county lacked statesmen and politicians. The greatest hero is our own John Hampden, the Patriot, who is still spoken of with affection. Close behind him is the popular Benjamin Disraeli, spending his youth at Bradenham and later living so happily at Hughenden. Buckinghamshire people very nearly burst with pride when he became Prime Minister. Yet another Prime Minister, the Duke of Portland lived at Gerrards Cross, and eloquent Edmund Burke at Beaconsfield. He founded a school at Penn for the orphans of those aristocrats who died during the French Revolution.

The county boasts its share of celebrated soldiers and sailors – Charles Cavendish, third Baron Chesham of Latimer, led the men of Bucks (the Yeomanry) in the Boer War. Admiral Howe of Penn defeated the French fleet on 'the glorious 1st of June' in 1794. And there is Sir Hugh Palliser of Chalfont St Giles, Commander of the British fleet at the Battle of Quebec, later appointed Governor of Newfoundland, and both friend and patron of Captain James Cook.

I could continue to describe the rich tapestry of Buckinghamshire history, but it is the unknown and unnoticed people, who have gone quietly about their work and toil through the centuries, that have shaped and made the county. They have supported the local industries, have farmed and worked the fields, driven their cattle into market. They are the men of the woods, the bodgers, the chairmakers, brickmakers, lacemakers, duckbreeders, strawplaiters – the generations that have replaced one another, century after century. They are the story and colour of the county.

In working with Andy Williams on this book, I acknowledge with thanks the assistance of Ivan Mills of Dunton Bros. Anything he does not know about bricks after forty-seven years in the trade is not worth knowing! Grateful thanks also go to many others who gave me help, including The Cliveden Hotel, Marg Dunton of Bellingdon, Rosalind Benfield of Marsh Gibbon and Meg Green.

Jean Archer
Amersham, July 1994

Turville and Hambleden

Turville, standing at the head of the Hambleden Valley, has often been called the prettiest village in the county, though this is a dangerous thing to say with the attractive villages of Fingest, Skirmett and Frieth in such close proximity. All four nestle in this lovely corner of the Chilterns, snug in their own fold of the hills. High above Turville stands a windmill once owned by Hayley Mills, the actress. It was used in the filming of *Chitty Chitty Bang Bang*.

Somehow, here at Turville, church, cottages, green and pub, the Bull and Butcher, all seem on a small scale and present the aspect of a dream village. The church has a squat 15th century tower and an exterior of knapped flint that is almost entirely Victorian.

This peaceful scene holds an ancient mystery. In the churchyard is a tomb, the last resting place of a 13th century priest, but when the coffin was opened in later years it was discovered that the priest had disappeared and instead inside there lay the remains of a woman who had been shot!

In the 19th century the 'Sleeping Girl of Turville' slumbered for nine years in one of the cottages near the church, fed by her mother with port wine and sugar and the aid of a teapot. On waking, although only managing to open one eye for some time, giving the impression of a permanent wink, she lived a normal

life and even married and had children.

The inset view on this page is of Hambleden Mill with its white walls reflected in the river. It is considered one of the most beautiful sights on the Thames, and has become a favourite calendar subject. It is thought to have been constructed around 1420 but there was a mill here at the time of Domesday, when the annual rent was just £1.

Marlow

Marlow is a most enchanting riverside town, its graceful suspension bridge side by side with the tall, proud steeple and spire of All Saints church. There are many buildings of historical and architectural interest in the town, a wide range of shops and a delightful tow-path walk. Add to that the beautiful setting of the rolling Chiltern Hills and woods, not to mention the river Thames, and you see why the poet Shelley and his wife, Mary, were drawn to live here.

The suspension bridge was built in 1831-6 to a design by William Tierney Clark. It replaced a wooden bridge built in 1789, which in turn had replaced an earlier bridge of 1294. Apparently, during the course of the last construction, Marlow was visited by a

Hungarian Count whilst enjoying a tour of Europe. The Count was filled with admiration and a short time later Clark was asked to construct the almost identical bridge that spans the Danube and links Buda with Pest.

Daniel Defoe visited the town in the 18th century and was amazed at 'the great embarkation of goods on the Thames at Marlow from the neighbouring towns', as well as 'the vast quantity of Beechwood from the woods in Buckinghamshire which was sent to the capital'.

Gazing down from the bridge into the broad, flowing river, edged with boathouses and gardens, there is a feeling of peace and tranquillity that is essentially Marlow and which has filled so many writers with inspiration. Certainly Shelley wrote freely here, and his wife wrote what was surely to become one of the best sellers of all time – *Frankenstein*, while their friend Thomas Love Peacock wrote *Nightmare Abbey*. Jerome K. Jerome wrote some of *Three Men in a Boat* here, reputedly in the Three Brewers.

Visitors flocked to the town in Victorian days and they still do, not only to see the Regatta in June, but also for the swan-upping which takes place in the first week in August.

The Compleat Angler affords a comfortable riverside retreat. It started life as a very small inn and acquired the name from Izaak Walton's book on angling which he wrote in and around Marlow in 1652.

Sheep graze safely and peacefully in the lush green meadows (*inset*) to the south of Marlow, with the spire of All Saints church in the background.

Cliveden

The glory of Cliveden is its position – over 200 feet up among wooded hills overlooking the winding river Thames. The views from the house are superb. In fact, the house and gardens are so poised over the river that the very name, 'Cliff-den', describes the cliff-like appearance of the river bank at this point.

In the 18th century, Frederick, Prince of Wales, father of King George III, used Cliveden as a country retreat and, at a masque held there in 1740 to celebrate the birthday of his daughter, the song *Rule Britannia* was played for the first time.

The first house, built for the 2nd Duke of Buckingham, was destroyed by fire, caused by a servant reading in bed; her candle caught the curtains. It was rebuilt in 1830 only to be burned down again in 1849.

The present house was built in 1851 from the design of Sir Charles Barry, architect of the Houses of Parliament, and it is said to be on a level with the terrace of Windsor Castle.

Further additions were made to the house in 1870 and then again in 1893 when the Astor family took over. Eventually it came to Waldorf Astor and his wife, Nancy, the first woman to take her seat in Parliament and one of the best known personalities of her time. She was a great hostess, entertaining many famous people at Cliveden. It became the centre for what was known as 'the Cliveden Set'. Their efforts to avoid the First World War were somewhat misconstrued.

During both World Wars it was used as a hospital and in 1942 the Astors gave Cliveden to the National Trust. It is now the only hotel in Britain that is also a stately home, and is set in 376 acres of private gardens and parkland.

The 1st Viscount Astor commissioned the 'Fountain of Love' (*inset*) from Thomas Waldo Story, an American sculptor.

Burnham Beeches

'We're going to Burnham Beeches to have a donkey ride!' So sang generations of excited children on every Sunday school outing from a wide area. In the 19th century they piled into waggonettes, which gradually as the years passed became small buses, and set off through the leafy lanes to picnic and play under the giant, grotesquely shaped beeches (they came by their weird shapes due to 300 years of pollarding for fuel) and to take that long-anticipated equestrian ride. Today, there are more amusements and the visitors are plentiful during the summer months. In the autumn the colours of the trees are breathtaking.

Formerly belonging to Burnham Abbey, Burnham Beeches comprises over 500 acres of beechwood that provides a happy habitat for all kinds of wild animals, birds and plants and is preserved for all time for the public at large.

All this is due to the foresight of a Victorian naturalist called Heath who suggested to the Corporation of London in 1880 that they purchase this area for the people of their city, and the general public, to enjoy. At that time there was a considerable amount of opposition from the locals, but this was soon overcome and today it would seem that they are proud of their woods which are now the most celebrated in Buckinghamshire. However, the many drives, walks and small paths that cross and recross make it easy to become lost.

There have been many visiting celebrities over the centuries, including the composer Mendelssohn, the poet Thomas Gray, and that expert woodsman, John Evelyn. There is the delightful tale that towards the end of the summer, the nightingales from all over the country come flocking to the Beeches and unite in a final concert before flying south.

Medmenham and the Hell Fire Club

It may be thought that people in high places today are prone to scandals, but in the latter part of the 18th century it was much worse. Half the Cabinet, peers, artists and even Royalty were involved in the orgiastic rites which took place at Medmenham Abbey where the notorious Hell Fire Club, founded by Sir Francis

Dashwood, held its meetings.

The Abbey was a Cistercian house founded in the 13th century, but not much is preserved of the old building. Sir Francis, who leased it for his club, made some additions and alterations.

Overlooking this pretty reach of the river Thames, the building today presents a picture of absolute peace with weeping willows and lawns running down to the water's edge, against a backcloth of wooded hills and deep valleys.

But those early members had a high old time with a plentiful wine cellar, chasing the girls from London brothels around the grounds and even endeavouring to evoke the Devil himself. They called themselves 'the Monks of Medmenham' and the ladies were called 'Nuns'.

Tales began to spread around the countryside of the goings-on until it all became a nationwide scandal and Sir Francis decided it was time to move the venue. Where better than the deep caves at West Wycombe where it was impossible for them to be overlooked, and where the orgies could continue undisturbed. And so the unbridled frolics went on. Today the caves are open to the public.

Sir Francis redesigned the church of St Lawrence on top of the hill at West Wycombe and capped it with a great golden ball, 100 feet above the ground, which serves as a landmark for miles around (*inset*). It is said that ten or twelve people can sit and drink comfortably in this orb. In fact, John Wilkes said 'it was the best Globe Tavern I ever was in'.

Beaconsfield

Beaconsfield, like Amersham, has an old and new town plus a wide street flanked with inns, old buildings and fine galleries. The old town is on the main road between Oxford and London, once the old coach road, and the church stands at the crossroads with a marvellous old rectory built in 1543. It is a town of 'Ends' – London End, Wycombe End, Aylesbury End and Windsor End.

In coaching days it was an important staging post, the Saracen's Head and the White Hart keeping a good supply of fresh horses on standby for when the coaches stopped for a change-over. The coach left London at 11 am, reached Beaconsfield at 1 pm and Oxford at 4 pm, and this was done at just a steady trot.

The heaths and woods around were a favourite haunt of highwaymen waiting for their prey. One was Jack Shrimpton, a local lad from Penn who 'made good' as a gentleman of the road, and another was the famous Claude Duval who broke all records by stealing 100 sovereigns from a local farmer.

Beaconsfield seems to draw famous people. The poet Edmund Waller, who lived at nearby Hall Barn, lies in the churchyard, the politician Edmund Burke lived at Gregories, and Benjamin Disraeli so loved the town that he chose to be Lord Beaconsfield when the time came. It was the same for writers – G.K. Chesterton, Enid Blyton, Alison Uttley, William Hickey, and Robert Frost, to name but a few.

In the new town, in Warwick Road, is the famous model village of Bekonscot (*inset*). Started by Roland Callingham in 1929, not only children are enthralled by its castles, churches, racecourse, zoo and villages. It has been visited by thousands over the years; it is open seven days a week in the summer from 10 am to 5 pm.

Jordans and William Penn

In this sequestered, wooded hollow in the heart of the Chilterns, some two miles from Beaconsfield, is the grave of William Penn (1644–1718), the founder of Pennsylvania. It draws visitors from across the Atlantic and all parts of the world year after year. He lies between his two wives, Gulielma and Hannah and several of his children. Gulielma (Guli) is said to have been attractive not only in looks but also in personality, and Penn courted her at Bury Farm in nearby Amersham.

Around him cluster the headstones of those early friends; Thomas Ellwood and his wife, Mary Ellis of Coleshill, Isaac and Mary Pennington, and others. They all lie in front of the most famous of Quaker Meeting Houses here at Jordans. It was built in 1688, when the passing of the Toleration Act allowed such buildings to be erected, with money donated by Mary Pennington. It is simplicity itself, of plain red brick with a hipped roof and includes a caretaker's cottage of two storeys, the actual meeting place consisting of one storey with a gallery on the upper floor. Adorning the walls are letters from those early pioneers who followed Penn to America. Seldom is such unforgettable peace experienced as in this quiet place.

Further up the slope is the Mayflower Barn, said to have been constructed with timbers from the *Mayflower*. It is both spacious and lofty and is a favourite venue for local events such as book sales, concerts etc.

Also in this complex owned by the Society of Friends is Old Jordans Farm built in the 17th century, which is now Old Jordans Guest Hostel and Conference Centre – just the place for rest and contemplation. It is available for private guests and is in no way limited to membership of the Society of Friends.

Little Missenden

The Missenden bypass, built in the 1950s, ensured that Little Missenden remains untroubled by too much modern traffic. As a result, the busy A413 rushes by just a few hundred yards from the peace of this pretty, tranquil village.

The church of St John the Baptist is one of the oldest in the Chilterns, and is well known for its impressive mural paintings, which were not discovered until 1931. The most striking is the one depicting St Christopher carrying the Christ child over a stream. The saint stands ten feet high, and in the rippling water around his feet swim an eel and a pike.

The source of the little river Misbourne is at Great Missenden and so it is in its early stages as it runs through Little Missenden, making its way through meadows to the back of the church, on past cottage gardens and the rear of the two pubs, the Red Lion and the Crown. It also runs through the gardens of the mellow, Jacobean manor house where once lived Dr Benjamin Bates (1730-1828), who was personal physician to Sir Francis Dashwood, the founder of the notorious Hell Fire Club. Bates was a member of the Club, often saying that its reputation was not as bad as it was painted.

Dr Bates was also a patron of the arts and numbered among his friends no less than Sir Joshua Reynolds, first President of the Royal Academy, who liked nothing better than to slip down to Little Missenden manor house in the company of his girlfriend, the Swiss artist Angelica Kauffman, for a weekend. Whilst there she designed the delightful terrace and gardens at the rear.

Little Missenden is at one end of the old traditional pathway from Amersham, where long ago families dressed in their best walked through Shardeloes Park, and refreshed themselves in the garden of the Crown before walking lazily back to Amersham.

Chenies Manor and Shardeloes

The splendidly tall, twisted chimneys of the Manor peep through the lofty branches of the trees at Chenies, a small village lying some three miles to the east of Amersham. On a hill overlooking the lovely Chess Valley, church, manor house and cottages cluster around a village green which has a roofed well and a pump. Henry VIII so admired those tall chimneys that he had them copied for his Palace at Hampton Court.

The Manor is thought to be early Tudor but is nowhere near the size of the house when it was visited by Queen Elizabeth I, who planted a tree. The building now consists of two wings, and is a joy to visit. It is said that some of the southern windows were blocked up during the time of the plague as it was thought the germs blew in from the south. Spacious rooms and colourful gardens, particularly the physic and Victorian gardens, create a nostalgia for bygone times.

The village was originally called Isenhampsted, after the 12th century lord of the manor, who was probably an ancestor of the Cheynes from whom the village undoubtedly gets its modern name. Some time later through marriage it passed to the famous Russell family and they owned it for four centuries, the house passing from them as late as 1954. It is open to the public on Wednesdays and Thursdays from 2 pm to 5 pm.

Over the hill at Amersham stands Shardeloes manor house (*inset*) but this is not open to the public as it is now divided into luxury flats. The Drake family were lords of the manor here for some 300 years and Shardeloes was built for Sir William Drake MP, in 1758-66 to a design by Stiff Leadbetter. Robert Adam also had a hand in it. The grounds were laid out by Humphrey Repton who dammed the river Misbourne to create the lake below the house.

Amersham

The tall, gaunt figure of John Knox, the Scottish Protestant reformer, strode through Amersham churchyard on 16th July 1553 to preach a sermon in the church in favour of Lady Jane Grey. His timing was bad. Some two days later, Mary Tudor attained the throne and poor little 16 year old Lady Jane was beheaded. It is not surprising that he left the country at speed.

The church dates from the 13th century, restoration taking place towards the end of the 19th century when the split flint covering was applied. It is renowned throughout the county for its fine monuments to the Drake family who were lords of the manor at Shardeloes for 300 years.

Amersham is a fascinating old market town with a wide High Street displaying many periods of architecture. The Market Hall was built in 1682 by Sir William Drake MP in the days when Amersham was a borough and returned two members to Parliament. The right to hold a market, together with a Whit Monday cattle fair and September fair, was granted by King John.

The market fell away during the 19th century, but is now held in a car park up at Amersham on the Hill on a Tuesday. The cattle fair ceased during the Second World War, but the fair still comes and colourfully straddles this old High Street.

High on the hill at the back of the church, overlooking the town, stands an obelisk monument to the Lollard martyrs of the Chiltern Hills, and in particular the five men and one woman of the town who were burned at the stake near that spot in 1521.

Many visitors come to old Amersham to stroll around the town and the pretty meadows at the back of the High Street.

The memorial gardens that abut onto the churchyard are a popular feature. They are dedicated to the dead of two World Wars and are beautifully maintained by the Amersham Town Council.

The King's Arms in the High Street (*inset*) was enlarged and renovated in the 1930s. The first public house was approximately half the size of the attractive building we see today. An early film based on the exploits of Dick Turpin was filmed here with Ronald Colman (the movie heart throb of the day) playing the lead.

Milton's Cottage

John Milton loved flowers:

'The tufted crow-toe and pale jessamine,
The white pinks and pansy freaked with jet
The glowing violet
The musk rose and the well-attired woodbine
With cowslips wan that hang the pensive head.'

So when, in 1665, with the plague raging in London, Thomas Ellwood at Chalfont St. Peter received a letter from his poet friend asking him to find a house in the area, he knew a garden to go with it would be important.

In his autobiography, Ellwood says 'I took a pretty box for him at Giles Chalfont, of which I gave him notice.' The Quakers in the locality were agog with excitement at the prospect of having this great man to live among them, but the sad thing was that when he arrived, there were none to welcome him. Thomas Ellwood, Isaac Pennington and others had been arrested whilst attending a Quaker funeral at Amersham, and thrown without much ceremony into Aylesbury Gaol.

They were released after a month, and Tom raced down to the 'pretty box' to greet Milton. Milton gave his friend the manuscript of his latest poem, asking him to take it home to read, which he did. It was *Paradise Lost*.

Milton and his family stayed in the 'pretty box' only ten months before returning to London early in 1666. The plague in London had begun to abate, and one or two cases had occurred in Chalfont St. Giles itself. There seemed little reason to stay.

On the opposite page is 'the pretty box' as it is today, with a garden full of flowers. The actual date of construction is unknown, but it is judged to be towards the end of the 16th century.

Over the years it passed through many hands until in 1887 a fund was set up locally, in order to purchase the cottage and dedicate it as a Museum to the memory of John Milton. Queen Victoria herself started things rolling with a subscription of £20. It is the only residence of his now remaining and people come from all parts of the world to see the many relics of the great man, which include valuable editions of his works – even a lock of his hair! The cottage is beautifully maintained, and the presence of the Poet seems to pervade those low-ceilinged rooms and twisting staircases.

Chesham Bois and Chesham

There can be no lovelier sight than a Chiltern wood in spring with its carpet of bluebells and dappled sunlight filtering through the trees. Happily, the extensive woods at Chesham Bois are under the knowledgeable management of the Woodland Trust, and stretch down to form a pleasant division between Amersham and Chesham.

Oddly enough, the name 'Bois' has nothing to do with the proliferation of woods, but derives from the Norman family of Du Boyes who owned the manor in the 13th century.

The village stands on a ridge – in the middle, the war memorial designed as a scroll, and a handful of shops and houses. Arthur Mee described the pretty little church of St Leonard as 'the church in the meadow', as it is approached by a long drive. Restored mostly in 1884, it stands on the site of a medieval church and contains some interesting monuments.

Very little development took place until this century when Metroland began to arrive. Larger houses appeared with spacious gardens and Chesham Bois became a very desirable place to live.

Although today it is often considered a part of Amersham, Chesham Bois has its own parish council. They look after the common, which skirts the Amersham-Chesham road, in an admirable manner. The pond was formed by the digging of clay for bricks.

Down below in the valley is the town of Chesham (*inset*) where the river Chess rises. The High Street has been pedestrianised and an attractive new clock tower was erected in 1992. The face or dial is that saved from the town's old 18th century Town Hall, which was demolished in 1969.

In 1845 a group of people met in an upstairs room of the old hall to form the Chesham Building Society. It is now the oldest surviving building society in the country, and its offices can be seen on the left of the picture.

High Wycombe

Benjamin Disraeli stood three times at High Wycombe as a Parliamentary candidate and was rejected at the polls each time! He even leaped up onto the porch of the Red Lion (now Woolworths) to deliver a passionate address to the electorate – all to no avail. He did eventually get elected at Maidstone; which is just as well, otherwise we should have missed one of the finest statesmen in our history. He loved the area, spending his youth at Bradenham, and purchasing Hughenden where he lived happily for many years.

High Wycombe is one of the largest towns in the county. It can certainly claim to have the largest parish church – the only one with a ring of twelve bells and a carillon. The High Street is wide with a Georgian aspect above modern shop fronts. Projecting out into the High Street, so that it more or less closes it, is the handsome, charming Guildhall, which was a gift to the town from the Earl of Shelburne in 1757. It is five-arched with an assembly room above.

Right opposite, in front of the church, is the interesting octagonal Market House, known as the 'Pepperpot' (*inset*). It has an open ground floor with heavy pillars and was first built in the 17th century and then rebuilt by Robert Adam in 1761.

High Wycombe was and is a chairmaking town and it has been claimed that 80% of all the chairs made in the country came from here. Nowhere near this figure could have been achieved without the help of the bodgers, who worked in the woods, turning out the legs for the chairs and keeping the factories plentifully and regularly supplied.

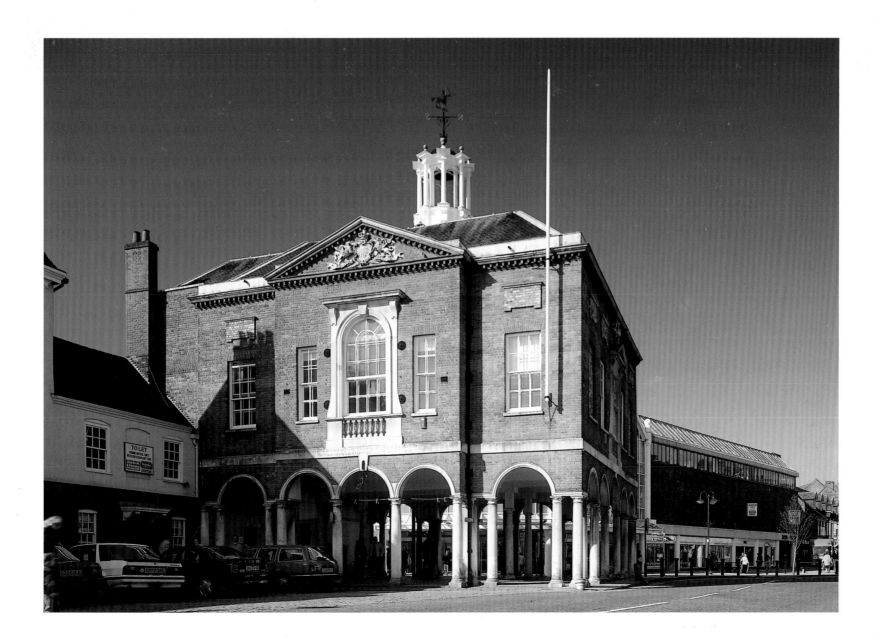

Lacey Green Windmill

In this secluded part of the Chilterns, the two villages of Lacey Green and Loosley Row appear to merge into one – Loosley Row halfway up the side of the valley and Lacey Green up on a long ridge.

This ridge stretches from Whiteleaf to eventually support a long, straight, open road from which views extend for miles over the Aylesbury Plain. Also from here can be obtained the best view of Grim's Dyke or Ditch, an ancient earthwork which crossed the Chilterns.

Standing back from this road, at its highest point, is a windmill, thought to be the oldest surviving smock mill and the third oldest mill in England. It was built in Chesham in 1650, moved to its present site in 1821, and it worked right up to 1917. It has been restored by the Chiltern Society and the machinery is probably original.

Poet Rupert Brooke (1887-1915) loved nothing more than walking in this part of the Chilterns with his jovial companions, and many times traversed that long, open road to his favourite inn, the Pink and Lily, that stands at the end. He wrote in his poem *The Chilterns*:

'I shall desire and I shall find
The best of my desires,
The autumn road, the mellow wind
That soothes the darkening shires,
And laughter and inn-fires.'

Hampden House

Hampden House sits in splendour overlooking the valley of Hampden Bottom in the countryside that John Hampden so loved. The house is much changed from his day; with its castellated roof, tall chimneys and porch it is now largely 18th century. However, the projection known as King John's Tower and parts of the interior are of the older building, including the great hall and gallery. It is approached by a long drive, a turning off the road to the village of Great Hampden, and the pretty church of St Mary Magdelene is just across the way.

The estates had been in the Hampden family since the Conquest. John's grandfather, old Griffith Hampden, entertained Queen Elizabeth I here at the house. Before she retired for the night, she complained it was a pity she could not see the view due to the great trees surrounding the house. During the night, Griffith had them chopped down, thus forming the majestic avenue, now known as The Queen's Gap, leading from the house down to the lodges at Hampden Bottom.

John Hampden (1594-1643) was a cousin of Oliver Cromwell and as the Civil War approached he represented first Wendover and then Buckinghamshire in Parliament. He was respected by other men and when he refused to pay King Charles the illegally levied Ship Money, others followed suit.

Later he played a leading role when Parliament passed the Grand Remonstrance, a condemnation of the King's misdeeds. This angered Charles and he attempted to arrest Hampden and four supporters for treason but they eluded him. It was at this time that 6,000 men of Buckinghamshire marched to London with petitions in his support.

He was killed at the battle of Chalgrove in 1643 and they brought his body back to this little church so close to his home. They carried him 'with their arms reversed, their drums and ensigns muffled and their heads uncovered'.

In the past few decades the house has been used as a school, and by Hammer Film Productions. It is now owned by an insurance company.

Ivinghoe Beacon

It goes without saying that the views and wide horizons seen from Ivinghoe Beacon, rising to nearly 800 feet above sea level, are truly magnificent. This is one of the highest peaks in the Chilterns. Grassy slopes roll away from it down to the Icknield Way. Sheep have kept the turf close cropped, allowing the chalk of the Chilterns to show through in paths and patches.

This is the beginning or end (depending on which way you look at it) of the Ridgeway Path, which was opened by the Countryside Commission in 1973 and runs the 85 miles from here to Overton Hill, near Marlborough, crossing the Thames at Goring.

At the summit, an indicator shows the visitor the principal places of interest visible. There are the Quainton Hills, the Lion cut in the chalk at Whipsnade, and countryside stretching from the borders of Bedfordshire across the Vale of Aylesbury to the heights of Ashendon and Brill – the whole a panorama of fields and woods of varying colours.

Ivinghoe Beacon is an Iron Age hill fort comprising nearly six acres surrounded by a single bank and ditch. A round barrow on the summit is of Bronze Age origin. True, it is not the largest in the county – that honour is given to Bulstrode Camp at Gerrards Cross – but it is the most important, as it is now believed to be one of the earliest in Britain. The advantage enjoyed by those early tribes of having a fort at such a high point is clearly to be seen.

The ancient and charming town of Ivinghoe lies to the west on the lower slopes. There is much of interest to see including a 16th century town hall, many old houses and inns, and a splendid church, which includes a Jacobean pulpit, an ancient hourglass and the most enthralling poppy-head bench ends.

The Vale of Aylesbury

From this point at Aston Clinton, the Vale of Aylesbury stretches away from the foothills of the Chilterns into the incredibly blue distance. A glorious sweep of fields, meadows, woods, farmhouses and ancient manor houses with cottages clustered around are all part of this rich, lush plain. Renowned for its fertility, which was ascribed to a preponderance of Kimmeridge clays, it was one of the finest dairy and stock-rearing areas in the whole of England. Certainly its produce filled the tables of Royalty since before Elizabeth I.

The antiquary, William Camden (1551-1623) described the fertility of the Vale in glowing terms. 'The rich meadows feed an incredible number of sheep, whose soft, fine fleeces are sought after, even from Asia itself. The beeves here pastured reach gigantic proportions, the sheep are not excelled in any part of the world, and the pigs are fed until they reach an enormous size.'

At one time every farm and village had its duck pond, for the Vale has been noted for duck breeding since early times. Elm trees were a particular feature of this countryside until the disastrous epidemic of Dutch Elm disease struck in the 1970s.

The rather long village of Aston Clinton lies on the A41. When Sir Anthony de Rothschild took over Aston Clinton House in 1851, it was the first home of the Rothschild family in the area. The house is now demolished and in the park is a training centre (Green Park) for the Youth and Community Service, run by the Buckinghamshire County Council.

Sir Anthony built two schools here in the 19th century, one of which has been demolished. The Anthony Hall erected in 1884 is still in full and constant use.

Ellesborough

It has been said, more than once, that Ellesborough church is haunted. Some say it is a rector who was here before the Civil War, and who has been seen walking up the church path. Others have said it is a mother and daughter who sit in a pew dressed in the fashion of the 1940s.

The church stands in an enviable position. Set up on a spur of the Chilterns against the vast backcloth of the Vale of Aylesbury, it looks grand from every direction. Dedicated to St Peter and St Paul, it is of flint and stone with a tall, battlemented tower and an even taller stair turret. Inside is the effigy of Bridget Croke 1683, who lies on her side in a rather uncomfortable position. There is also a portrait brass of Thomas Hawtrey in Tudor armour.

The whole area is full of footpaths that provide the most delightful walks. On the hills in spring, the short, green turf is covered with cowslips and violets, especially when skirting the Chequers estate, which is in the parish of Ellesborough.

Chequers has provided a retreat for Prime Ministers since 1921 when Lord Lee of Fareham donated it to the nation for that specific purpose. Most, if not all, of those occupying this high office during that time have attended Ellesborough church, together with countless foreign dignitaries and Royalty.

The house is set in one of the most beautiful basins of the Chilterns. Above it looms Coombe Hill, with its monument to the dead of the Boer War and, just behind, the hills rise to over 900 feet, the highest point in the range.

The little path opposite the church leads to Beacon Hill and Cymbelines Mount, and down here nestle the tiny almshouses founded by Dame Dodd's charity under a will of 1746.

Wendover

Robert Louis Stevenson, on a walking tour of the Chilterns in 1875, called it 'a straggling, purposeless sort of place'. What was he talking about? Wendover is a delightful town, and an ideal place from which to explore the Chilterns, the Ridgeway and the Aylesbury Plain.

It lies on a curve of the ancient Upper Icknield Way, against a backcloth of hills rising to over 800 feet covered with canopies of beechwoods. In the Chiltern Forest, the Forestry Commission has laid out nature trails, and, on the other side of this gap, Coombe Hill, with its

impressive monument to those men of the county who fell in the Boer War, stands out against the skyline for miles, affording fantastic views over the Aylesbury Plain.

The mellow brick and thatched cottages in Aylesbury Street form a superb frontage, and any modern infilling in the town has been done with care. There are some fine old inns. Stevenson stayed at the Red Lion and perhaps tried to make amends by recording that he 'never saw any room to be more admired than the low wainscoted parlour' in which he spent the evening. Oliver Cromwell also stayed here, as did Rupert Brooke.

Wendover was once a Borough and returned to Parliament such distinguished representatives as John Hampden, Richard Steele, Edmund Burke and George Canning.

Most visitors remark on the elegant clock tower facing the oncoming traffic at the bottom of the High Street (inset). This was given to the town by Abel Smith in 1843. In May 1950 the people thought they might have lost it, when a freak tornado came hurtling down from the hills and laid parts of Wendover waste. A massive elm crashed through the churchyard wall, narrowly missing the clock tower and blocking the road.

Over the years, Wendover has become well used to seeing lads in Air Force blue walking its streets. Nearby is Halton, the estate once owned by Alfred de Rothschild. During the First World War he allowed part of his land to be used by the Royal Flying Corps. On his death the whole estate was taken over by the Royal Air Force, and is now an important RAF base and training ground.

Aylesbury

Aylesbury is the county town – the seat of the Assizes and administration. A fact that is there for all to behold with the tall building of the offices of the Buckinghamshire County Council, eleven storeys high, towering over the town and to be seen for miles. Once a town of old inns, nooks and crannies, now the oldest and most picturesque part of Aylesbury is at the 15th century King's Head at the top of the Market Square, and in the area of the church, most of which is Georgian.

The impressive building of the County Hall looks majestically up the Market Square. Built to a design approved by Sir John Vanbrugh (1664-1726), works are said to have started as early as the 1720s, but due to many hold ups (some political) it was not completed until 1740, long after his death. After a disastrous fire in 1970, the Court Room on the first floor has been restored to its 18th century grandeur with galleries, box pews and a judge's seat, behind which is a cupboard for his chamberpot!

The great arch next to the Hall is part of a former Corn Exchange of 1864, which unfortunately replaced the White Hart Inn, said to have been one of the most memorable hostelries outside London. It stood right next to the county gaol and was convenient for affluent prisoners to obtain their beer. The arch now leads to the Judge's Lodgings. Tucked in this corner is the Barber's Shop (*inset*) which adjoins a pub called the Grapes.

The statue of the 3rd Lord Chesham stands with impressive bearing at the bottom of the Square. He died in 1907 after a glittering military career, serving first with distinction in India. On his retirement he became the

Colonel of the Bucks Hussars whereupon he organised an entirely new force of Bucks Yeomanry. During the Boer War, in command of the Tenth Battalion containing two Bucks companies, he set out for South Africa where he was given command of the whole Yeomanry Brigade.

Aylesbury – Market Square

Every Wednesday, Friday and Saturday, Aylesbury Market Square is filled with brightly coloured stalls and booths, and the cries of vendors, just as it has been through the centuries although the town did not receive its Charter until 1553, which was quite late compared with other towns in the county. The tall, 70 feet high clocktower raises its head above all the bustle and activity. In 1876 it replaced a small market house, which in turn had replaced an 'ancient dirty' market house built on oak pillars, where cockfighting and badger baiting went on, and conjurors and fortune tellers performed in the upper room.

The town seems to spread out from the Market Square, the heart of Aylesbury, where stand the county's favourite heroes, John Hampden, Benjamin Disraeli and the third Lord Chesham. It slopes gently down from the Kings Head at the top to the County Hall at the bottom.

The 15th century Kings Head, now owned by the National Trust, is tucked behind buildings of a later date and reflects that wonderful old Aylesbury, little of which now remains. The Inn is steeped in history. Its windows include stained glass commemorating the marriage of Henry VI and Margaret of Anjou; it is said they spent their honeymoon here.

The Square has seen many momentous occasions for it was here that the people gathered in past moments of crisis and celebration, such as the arrival of the stage coach in 1815 that carried the news of the great victory at Waterloo. And on 18th June 1839 the people seemed to go mad with joy at the opening of their little railway line to Cheddington, thus linking Aylesbury with the London-Birmingham line.

There were the fun and frolics of the elections and, more sadly, there were tearful goodbyes for apprehensive men and women gathered before setting off as emigrants for a new life in America or New South Wales.

Watermead Village

Just to the north of Aylesbury, off the A413 road to Buckingham, and before the village of Hardwick, stands the brand new purpose-built village of Watermead.

Reached by its own single road access both in and out, it comprises some 200 acres, with 120 acres of lake and parkland which is alive with birds of many varieties. It consists of around 800 houses, all individually designed and in varying colours. When approached it is almost as if a colourful city is rising from the plain ahead, its reflection glittering in the windsurfing and sailing lake.

On first entering the approach, the 40-bed hotel is on the right and a ski slope on the left. Drive on and it seems that every facility has been provided for, from the Watermead Inn to a 50-bed nursing home at the lake's edge. There is a leisure centre, community hall, tennis courts and all-weather bowling. A bandstand on an island marks where concerts take place in summer.

It was in 1987 that planning permission was granted, as the Aylesbury Vale District Council saw an opportunity to add amenity and parkland adjacent to the town to fulfil the need for the fast growing sports of windsurfing and sailing. Since then thousands of trees, all local species, have been planted and what was once marshy farmland has been transformed into a quiet park, ideal for walking and jogging. It has become the home of the annual National Sprint Triathalon.

Today, the summer visitor can see the Watermead Cricket Club on their own cricket green, or simply walk among the trees and wild flowers.

Waddesdon Manor

Waddesdon Manor was built for Baron Ferdinand de Rothschild to a design by the French architect, Gabriel-Hyppolyte Destaileur, during the years 1874-1889. The terraces, gardens, roads and plantations were laid out by another Frenchman, Laine.

The Baron had fallen in love with the view from the top of Lodge Hill (*inset*). He thought the rich pastureland and ancient farms and manor houses of the Aylesbury Vale delightful, and it so happened that the estate of Waddesdon and Winchendon was up for sale. The Baron wanted a mansion of style where he could

invite his many distinguished friends to view his collections of art and other treasures.

He employed as much local labour as possible to help in the building. The Bath stone used in the construction was transported by steam tram. He insisted that mature trees should be planted and special carts had to be made to carry them, while Percheron horses pulled the heavy loads. The locals stood open-mouthed as all this activity took place and the carts passed through their village.

The village of Waddesdon blossomed and took on a new lease of life. The Baron built a new village hall, hotel, reading room and cottages. Many of the buildings bear the Rothschild insignia of five arrows bound together with a coronet. This represents the original five brothers who left Frankfurt in the early 19th century, and the grant of a baronetcy to the family by the Vienna College of Heralds in 1822.

The grounds of the house are extensive and include an aviary. The Baron moved in and was soon entertaining such elevated guests as the Prince of Wales, who stayed there frequently, and Queen Victoria, who made a day of it on 14th May 1890. But the Baron's enjoyment of his house was short-lived for he died in 1898 and his sister, Alice, inherited. From her it passed to James de Rothschild who bequeathed it to the National Trust, thus enabling people from all over the world to enjoy this wonderful building and its treasures.

Haddenham and Long Crendon

An extensive village with wide streets and narrow alleys, Haddenham is only three miles from Thame along the Aylesbury road. The focal point is Church End Green where the large pond laps against churchyard walls overlooked by the 13th century parish church. An attractive lychgate adds to the charm of the scene, and the whole is surrounded by thatched and whitewashed cottages.

Here at Haddenham, the local building material known as 'wychert' (white earth) has been used not only for the construction of cottages, but also stables, cowsheds, meeting houses and walls. The walls were either tiled or thatched to stop the wet from going down into the clay. The pond played an important part in duck-rearing for the famous Aylesbury duck industry. In fact, the village was always called 'Silly' Haddenham as it was said the walls at the pond were thatched to keep the ducks dry!

Manorial courts were at one time held at the Green Dragon, one of the popular pubs – a green dragon being the emblem of the Earls of Pembroke who had authority here after the Reformation. This may account for the fact that there are a considerable number of dragons depicted in the church.

The Court House at nearby Long Crendon (*inset*), with its stone base and oversailing upper floor, was one of the first buildings to be owned and restored by the National Trust. Originally a wool store or staple hall, the timber frame is infilled with brick, wattle and daub. Manorial courts were first held here during the reign of

Henry V; later the Warden and scholars of All Souls at Oxford met here.

The Court House is to be found close by the church at the end of a High Street filled with quaint, picturesque cottages, pubs, and an old fashioned butcher's shop.

Brill

Standing next to the old windmill, at this famous viewpoint 700 feet above sea level, it feels as if you are perched on the very edge of the world and could step off to fly over the countryside that lies in all directions – over Aylesbury to Calvert and over Oxfordshire to the Cotswolds.

Pictures are plentiful of the windmill, which stands stark against the skyline; the soft, green turf of the hillocks around it usually covered with sheep. This uneven ground is said to be not only the remains of fortifications constructed during the considerable activity that took place here during the Civil War, but also the result of clay workings over several centuries. Villagers once had the right to graze their sheep here, and so stood out against a proposal for the ground to be levelled as they thought this would reduce the area of grass.

The post mill, complete with sails, was built in 1688. It is weatherboarded with a brick-protected base. The gears and millstones in the main chamber could be manipulated to suit the direction of the wind. It remained in use right up to 1916 and owes its survival to a local landowner. It is now in the care of the Buckinghamshire County Council.

Brill is of Saxon origin. Edward the Confessor is said to have had a palace here, and there was even a Norman castle. No trace remains of either. Once a part of the Forest of Bernwood, both William the Conqueror and Henry VIII are reputed to have hunted here.

Tram Hill was the terminus of the old Brill Tramway, which was connected with the main line at Quainton Road station and became one of the outposts of the Metropolitan Railway until it closed in 1935.

Cuddington and Nether Winchendon

The ancient village of Cuddington looks down from a limestone ridge over the river Thame. Consequently, the church is built of local limestone; it is 12th century, but was enlarged and altered all of four times during the 13th century, and restored by G.E. Street in the 19th.

In the churchyard wall (also of limestone) is a plaque set up by the Medical Officer of Health in 1849 to the memory of the 48 people, out of the 50 residing at nearby Gibraltar, who lost their lives 'due to Asiatic Cholera'.

Seen from the churchyard, the imposing and attractive Tyringham House has the date 1609 over the door. This is 'wychert' country where a white clay mixture is found, sometimes only three to four feet beneath the surface. Mixed with straw, it has been used as a building material. The 'wychert' cottages are durable, cosy and attractive and there are many in Cuddington.

Down in the valley below the village, in the quiet water meadows of the river Thame, lies the small, unforgettable village of Nether Winchendon (*inset*). Here the 'wychert' cottages are ochre-washed to show that they belong to the Bernard Estate. Amazingly, the little church of St Nicholas, with its blue and gold clock face, unlike that of Cuddington, has undergone absolutely no restoration or alterations since the 17th century. The tiny green is not adorned with any impressive memorial, timepiece or statue, but a wonderful old Victorian letter-box.

Nether Winchendon House is Tudor with 18th century additions, and has been the home of the Spencer Bernard family for generations. It is open to the public at certain times.

Quainton and Oving

At the top of the sloping green at Quainton is the base and shaft of this 15th century market cross, which is one of only a few to survive to this extent. It was a favourite place for villagers to gather, and from its steps many a proclamation has been read. Nearby, behind the cottages, stands the tower windmill, built in 1830 with bricks made on the site. Over 65 feet high, it is the tallest in the county and has six floors.

The charming almshouses were founded in 1687 by Richard Winwood, Secretary of State to James II, and

form an attractive group with their diagonally placed chimneystacks, dormer windows and Dutch gables. Add to that a variety of Tudor and 17th century cottages, with a dash of Georgian houses, and you have the enchantment of Quainton.

This idyllic village is particularly noted by all county historians as the birthplace of George Lipscombe in 1773. His great labour of love, *The History and Antiquities of the County Of Buckingham,* has pride of place in every reference library in the county. Unfortunately, he died a year before his book was published in 1847, having impoverished himself in the process.

Approximately one mile away to the south along the road to Waddesdon is the former Quainton Road station, which was closed in 1935. It is now the site of the Quainton Railway Centre where there is exhibited one of the country's largest collections of engines and rolling stock, including the Great Western's *King Edward I.*

Oving (*inset*) stands on a hill affording magnificent views over the countryside. It is a pretty village with church, manor house, green and the cheerful Black Boy Inn.

Winslow

Entering this delightful little town on the A413 from Aylesbury, you pass along an interesting street with picturesque cottages that leads up to the pleasing Market Square, before turning right to carry on to Buckingham.

Here at the heart of Winslow are two rambling old inns – the 18th century George Hotel, which has a wrought-iron balcony said to have come from Claydon House, and the Bell Hotel first mentioned at the beginning of the 17th century. Cromwell's men were billeted here during the Civil War, and there are romantic legends of Dick Turpin. Winslow has grown, as have most other places, and yet it has managed to preserve its old atmosphere and the lovely surrounding countryside.

Overlooking the varying roofs of the town stands Winslow Hall, built in 1700 for William Lowndes, Secretary to the Treasury (1695-1724). He was affectionately known as 'Ways and Means' Lowndes, due to a phrase he coined whilst executing his duties in that post. Winslow Hall was to all intents and purposes designed by Sir Christopher Wren as he not only checked the accounts but also trimmed the bills. Mr Lowndes spared no expense – over a million local bricks were used and three of the workmen had previously aided Wren in the construction of St Paul's Cathedral. Not only that, the woodwork was executed by the King's joiner and carpenter, and the gardens laid out by the Royal gardener. It is a dignified and impressive building.

Near the Market Square is the tiny Baptist chapel of Benjamin Keach, dated 1695. Before the chapel was built Keach was in trouble. He was a man way ahead of his time. He may not have foreseen sports and shopping being allowed on a Sunday, but he saw no reason whatsoever why children should not be allowed to relax and enjoy themselves on that day, and he published a book saying so. He paid dearly for this idea, was fined £20 and forced to stand in the pillory not only at Winslow but also at Aylesbury, presumably on a weekday!

Buckingham

Buckingham was once the county town. Alfred the Great decided it should be so in AD 888 when England was divided into shires; it was old enough and it was mentioned in the *Anglo Saxon Chronicle*. But over the centuries the county stretched and developed, especially in the south, and what with bad roads and poor communication, Aylesbury came to be considered far more central and convenient. By the 16th century, administration and status had been transferred to that town.

There was no doubt this caused some bad feeling – after all, Buckingham had given its name to the county. Efforts were made in the 18th century to recover at least the Summer Assizes, but the argument against this was that Buckingham had no gaol. It was then that Viscount Cobham of Stowe leaped into the breach and rapidly, at his own expense, erected in 1748 what is now known as the Old Gaol (*inset*). The building included a gaoler's house. It is now a museum. The south front was added in the same style by Gilbert Scott in 1839. It did the trick and the Summer Assizes returned to Buckingham, but only for a short time.

Buckingham is mainly a Georgian town, having been largely rebuilt after a disastrous fire in 1725. It has a wide main street similar to Amersham and Beaconsfield and there are many interesting buildings. The parish church, perched on a hill overlooking the town, is built on the site of a former castle. The old church practically fell down and was rebuilt in 1780. Later it was much restored by Scott.

Buckingham is proud of its University, for which a Royal Charter was granted in 1983. It is attended by students from all over the world.

Thornborough Bridge and Nash

Built of local stone during the 14th century, this is the only medieval bridge of its type in the county. It is 165 feet long and 12 feet wide and has six arches, three of which are ribbed. It spans the Claydon brook, a tributary of the river Ouse, as it runs gently through the flat, lush meadows of local farmland, overflowing here and there as it goes.

The bridge also supports the old boundary stone of Thornborough with Buckingham and gives way to small embrasures where people can stand and look down into the moving waters. It has happily carried traffic of all shapes and sizes for centuries, until modern-day drivers became exasperated with its narrowness. In recent years a new bridge was built a short distance upstream, allowing the busy A421 to bypass the old one, so as to ensure its preservation for posterity.

Nearby will be seen two huge earth mounds which will completely mystify the beholder. These are Roman burial mounds which were opened by the Duke of Buckingham around 1840. It is a wonder that curiosity was allayed so long! They were found to contain the richest series of Romano-British remains explored up until that date. Among the finds were Roman coins, the hilt of a sword, a small bronze lamp with its wick still in place, and an ornament of the purest gold. The sheer opulence of these artefacts is thought to reveal the presence of a local aristocracy at that time, and hence the great importance of the bridge and Thornborough itself.

Thornborough has been a farming community since before Domesday and the village is roughly one mile away from the bridge.

Close by is the tiny village of Nash (*inset*), which was made a separate parish from Thornton in 1894. It has a small church designed by G.E. Street and quaint, thatched cottages set in colourful gardens.

The Three Locks and Stony Stratford

It was the Duke of Bridgewater who started it all when he commissioned James Brindley to build the first canal in 1759. This was a brilliant idea that quickly caught on. Within 40 years of the opening of his waterway, no less than 165 applications had been made for cutting canals in Great Britain.

The Grand Union Canal from London to

Birmingham, which travels through Buckinghamshire, was projected in 1792, but not completely finished until 1805. It became a vital link between London and the industrial might of the Midlands. Starting at Brentford, it joins the Oxford Canal at Braunston. As it makes its way up through the county, there are several 'arms' or branches – one at Wendover, another at Aylesbury.

Near Stoke Hammond, some three miles from Bletchley, there are three locks on the Grand Union, which were installed in 1800. They have been improved and enlarged over the years, and bring the canal level down by 20 feet.

At the foot of the three locks there stands an old pub, much enlarged, and not surprisingly named the Three Locks. It is filled with interesting canal mementoes and memorabilia, bills and posters. Here people gather on a summer's day to watch the canal boats go through, and to stroll along the tow-path.

There are two inns at Stony Stratford with a coaching history. The Cock (*inset*) was first mentioned before 1500. The other is the Bull. It is said that because of the garbled versions of stories that came to them from the London coaches, the phrase 'a Cock and Bull story' came about.

Milton Keynes

Alison Uttley wrote of Milton Keynes in 1950 'a quiet village among the water meadows...a little place of thatch and farm house, with a 14th century church.' Seventeen years later, in 1967, Milton Keynes was designated to become Britain's first New City with 22,000 acres of land (34 square miles) made available to accommodate a population of 250,000 by the end of the century.

It incorporates the towns of Bletchley, Wolverton and Stony Stratford and thirteen villages such as Simpson and Woolstone, each retaining its own individuality. The responsibility for this growth and establishment lies with the Milton Keynes Development Corporation, which, from the outset was determined that the new city, whilst becoming one of the country's leading industrial centres, should also be aware of the past. Thus several sites of archaelogical importance have been preserved. There is a museum at Stacey Hill and another at Bradwell Abbey Field Centre, which is on the site of a 12th century Benedictine Priory. The city is divided by a grid pattern of roads and Central Milton Keynes is at the heart of it, containing the Civic Offices and Library together with an 80 feet high mirror glazed ziggurat containing the central railway station and Business and Entertainment Centre.

Many areas have been kept as 'green lungs', such as Willen Lake which has a conservation area and a nature trail. The lake is overlooked by the Japanese Buddhist 'peace pagoda' (*inset*). This is the first to be built in the western hemisphere.

The Grand Union Canal flows through the City and has been put to good use with canalside walks. As Christmas draws near, people from all parts of Buckinghamshire and beyond arrive at Milton Keynes shopping centre. It is one of the largest in Europe, with over 140 shops, and the Christmas displays and decorations are always created with a high degree of skill and imagination.

Newport Pagnell

Samuel Pepys said it was like a cathedral, and he was not far wrong. The church of St Peter and St Paul at Newport Pagnell is set on a slight rise above the river Ousel which, after running through the town, joins the river Ouse.

It is the largest church in this part of the county, and is mostly 14th century. The broad tower, however, was built in the 16th century and, rare in Buckinghamshire, the pinnacles are a Victorian embellishment. There is a priest's room above the vaulted roof of the north porch, fronting onto the High Street, and another porch has 14th century arcading where wooden corbels with grotesque faces support the 15th century roof.

Perhaps now too close to the M1 for comfort, the town still manages to retain much of its original character. Centuries ago it held an important position controlling the roads to the north. Both sides during the Civil War were of the opinion that its occupation was vital. It was first occupied by the Royalists, until Cromwell's army forced them out and it became a strong Parliamentary garrison under the governorship of Sir Samuel Luke. A 16 year old lad by the name of John Bunyan came to serve under him.

Oliver Cromwell could not have had happy memories of Newport Pagnell for it was here that his second son, Oliver, died of smallpox in 1644. He had been the 'apple of his father's eye' and was only 21 at the time of his death.

Beside the river can be seen the remains of the 13th century Tickford Abbey, and the road out to the south crosses the river at Tickford Bridge, the oldest cast-iron bridge still in use by traffic in the country, possibly the world.

Olney

The pinnacled tower and tall, stone spire of Olney's 14th century parish church are dominant and imposing over miles of the north Buckinghamshire countryside. The church stands on the banks of the tranquil, slow-moving river Ouse among willows and reeds in quiet water meadows. Grotesque heads adorn the pinnacles and beneath the parapet of the chancel are an assortment of faces with a variety of expressions – some happy, some sad.

In 1884 the top of the steeple was restored under the direction of Sir George Gilbert Scott, and the weathercock was taken down for regilding. On it was stamped the date 1829 and the words: 'I never crow, but stand to show where winds do blow.' As a bullet was found in the tail, the urge to crow must have been acute. In 1950, it was taken down again and this time several bullet holes were found.

John Newton was curate here from 1764 to 1780, having given up his life at sea. It was he who was responsible for bringing the poet William Cowper to live in Olney, where the two men jointly wrote the 'Olney Hymns' that are still popular today, among them *Amazing Grace*. The house where Cowper lived is now a museum, open during the summer months.

Despite a disastrous series of fires in the 19th century, Olney High Street and Market Place present one of the best preserved 18th century towns in the county. It was once the centre of the Buckinghamshire lace industry and in the town is to be found a lace factory built in 1909.

The Olney Pancake Race is still run every Shrove Tuesday from the Market Place to the churchyard gate.

Stowe

In 1680 Sir Richard Temple built himself a house at Stowe, smaller than the central block of the present house. When he died in 1697 it passed to his son, Richard, Viscount Cobham, who embarked upon making Stowe the ultimate in architectural and landscape design.

A three mile avenue leads from the town of Buckingham to the great park, which is a mixture of styles that make up a complete whole. Great names such as Vanbrugh and Kent had a field day and

'Capability' Lancelot Brown, starting work here as a young gardener, later completed the work and vision of Kent. William Cowper, living at Olney, wrote of Brown, the 'omnipotent magician':

'Lo, he comes . . .
Down falls the venerable pile,
'He speaks – the lake in front becomes a lawn;
Woods vanish, hills subside, and valleys rise.'

In fairness, it was before Brown's time that the village of Stowe was removed. Lord Cobham wished to do the same with the church, but was frustrated. The ecclesiastical authorities refused to allow it, so he planted trees in order to conceal it and the old church remains in the park.

Cobham's nephew, Lord Temple, inherited at his death and carried on the work of his uncle. He altered the north front of the house and had the south front completely remodelled to a design by Robert Adam. In 1882 the Temples were created Dukes of Buckingham.

The great Corinthian arch is an impressive introduction to those fabulous acres of grottoes, follies and temples, not to mention the Palladian Bridge, Elysian Fields, Temple of Worthies and many other innovations which delight the eye. Stowe is a place of international importance. It is a glorious expanse created by a glittering array of great names in design.

In 1923 Stowe was opened as a new public school and remains so to this day.

Dunton Brothers' Brickworks

Much of the county of Buckinghamshire has lacked the necessary stone that could be quarried for building purposes; some often had to be imported from neighbouring counties. But a variety of clays was plentiful, and consequently the predominant building material in Bucks became brick, which gradually replaced the timber frame infill of wattle and daub. Tiles were produced from medieval times at places such as Penn and Tylers Green where they supplied many local churches, not to mention the Palace of Westminster and even Windsor Castle.

On the slopes of the Chilterns in particular, a wealth and diversity of clay is to be found. In cottages and houses bricks are omnipresent and often used on church towers. Around Bellingdon, Chesham and Cholesbury clay has been extracted that enables bricks to be made in a wide variety of colours.

A primitive method of discovering whether a particular field would reveal clay was used well into this century. All that was needed was a metal rod and a bucket of water. The water softened the crust of the earth and the rod was used as a probe. If the result was favourable, extraction took place with the aid of a windlass, which brought up buckets of clay loaded by men down below. Shouts of unbridled reproach were heard from the depths if any buckets wavered and discharged the contents back from whence they came.

Such was the method used by six brothers by the name of Dunton. In 1937 they found clay on a piece of land at Bellingdon End owned by their mother, and scraping together all the money they could find, they started the firm of Dunton Brothers. They worked hard making by hand the now famous Chesham Multis and Greys, but in 1939 war was declared, and this meant that brickmaking came to an abrupt halt due to air raid precautions. The firing of a brick kiln could last for days and at night could easily be seen from above by enemy aircraft. The six brothers were engaged on wartime employment until the end of the war, when they re-united and began brickmaking once again.

By 1949 clay was exhausted at the Bellingdon site and they opened up another at Cholesbury until that too ran out. They moved to the site at Ley Hill in 1952. The brothers sold their interest in 1974, yet still today the firm of Dunton Bros. produces first class bricks of all colours, shapes and sizes to cater for a continuing demand.

Marsh Gibbon

There are not many buildings remaining in the county as well preserved as this Elizabethan Manor House at Marsh Gibbon. Built of stone with high gables, it is thought to date from around 1560. The Hall, which occupies the ground floor of the central block, is approached through a porch with a stone moulded archway. Inside is an original wide stone fireplace with a four-centred arch, and it is not difficult to imagine a blazing fire crackling away in winter.

It was the Manor House of the Crokes and, after the death of Alexandra Croke in 1757, it was converted into a farmhouse, which is its present function.

The village of Marsh Gibbon lies to the south-west of Twyford, and so close to the border of Oxfordshire that it is only some four miles from Bicester. It can be traced back to Edward the Confessor when it was called Merse, the name Gibbon coming from a family that held lands here at the time of King John. The manor eventually came into the ownership of the De la Poles who founded an almshouse at Ewelme in 1437, granting the manor as part of its endowment.

In 1740 the village suffered a disastrous fire in which over thirty houses were destroyed and, by the next century, the result of the fire made the village look devastated and derelict. In 1860, the Master of Ewelme visited the village and decided to liven things up. He built rows of cottages and gave the village a water supply and reading room.

Marsh Gibbon can boast one of the oldest Friendly Societies still in existence. The Greyhound Club derives its name from the Greyhound Inn in the village and today there are around 160 members. The Club Feast Day is on Oakapple Day and includes a march to the Church with flags flying.